Praise for
Oh Witness L

"*Oh Witness Dey!* reminds us that we see through the eyes of past generations as readers and as people of the Americas. These poems remind us of the importance of looking back, because history defines our present and our future, as the past is not past, and the greed and violence echo down generations. Shani Mootoo's voice captures that echo and yet transmutes it, elevates it into song. *Oh Witness Dey!* fuses emotional momentum with discursive energy, which is underscored by carefully researched knowledge of colonial practices dating back to Columbus. The story of how Europe's rapacity accelerated in the wake of 'discovery' is timely and inexhaustible, and these poems bear impassioned witness to a world that has raced past its precipice."
—Kaie Kellough, Griffin Poetry Prize-winning author of
   Magnetic Equator

"A formidable, bold, and expansive collection of poetry that highlights Shani Mootoo's aesthetic and intellectual prowess. Rich in luminous detail, *Oh Witness Dey!* is an unflinching exploration of colonial histories, one that opens up space for supple, nuanced insights."
—Linda Morra, writer/host, *Getting Lit With Linda*

Praise for
Cane | Fire

"A powerful and deeply intelligent confrontation of self and what is
sustained in the embers."
—Madhur Anand, author of *Parasitic Oscillations*

"From the first exquisite poems to the collection's lyrical and vulnerable
culmination, Mootoo undertakes a daunting and necessary vision: to
extricate personal history and recast it."
—Doyali Islam, author of *heft*

"*Cane | Fire* is a testament to the multi-skilled novelist, poet, and artist
that Shani Mootoo is."
—*Minola Review*

"Holding this book and experiencing the way the art is laid out on the
page was a true experience by itself."
—*The Miramichi Reader*

"Employing the glittering detail and a mythic tone that characterizes
her fiction, Mootoo has crafted a poetic memoir that reimagines
her family histories, including journeys from Ireland to Trinidad and
Canada."
—*Quill & Quire*

"Mootoo's artworks, most of which feature some sort of collage and
reassembly, shift the effects of memory, of line, of sound, of relation
and amplify the transformative possibilities of these poems."
—*Winnipeg Free Press*

OH
WITNESS
DEY!

OH WITNESS DEY!

Shani Mootoo

POEMS

Book*hug Press
Toronto 2024

Library and Archives Canada Cataloguing in Publication
Title: Oh witness dey! / Shani Mootoo.
Names: Mootoo, Shani, author.
Description: Poems.
Identifiers: Canadiana (print) 20230481302 | Canadiana (ebook) 20230481329
  ISBN 9781771668767 (softcover)
  ISBN 9781771668781 (PDF)
  ISBN 9781771668774 (EPUB)
Classification: LCC PS8576.O622 O4 2024 | DDC C811/.54—dc23

The production of this book was made possible through the generous assistance of
the Canada Council for the Arts and the Ontario Arts Council. Book*hug Press also
acknowledges the support of the Government of Canada through the Canada Book
Fund and the Government of Ontario through the Ontario Book Publishing Tax Credit
and the Ontario Book Fund.

Book*hug Press acknowledges that the land on which we operate is the traditional
territory of many nations, including the Mississaugas of the Credit, the Anishnabeg,
the Chippewa, the Haudenosaunee, and the Wendat peoples. We recognize the
enduring presence of many diverse First Nations, Inuit, and Métis peoples, and are
grateful for the opportunity to meet, work, and learn on this territory.

Book*hug Press

For all those in whose veins oceans flow

foremost among them my dear friends
Richard Fung and Tim McCaskell

Contents

We

Wondrous Cold

Cosmic

Notes

Acknowledgements

About the Author

Descendants of the dust of the old

We, of the new, of the now

Our ancestors survived

Even the bubonic plague

Praise Be

Praise Be

There is no racing
Past the backs
Of Samarsingh and Bulaki
What point pulling hair, digging dirt
With DNA shovels?
Fingernails scraping columns
Of a ship's registry
Entertaining fantasies of brotherhood
Forged in the house-home
Of a stinking hull
An emptying well
Just a(s) well

My ancestry is the Big Bang
My ancestry is pepper and spice
My ancestry is a Spanish Queen
My ancestry is a Genoese navigator
My ancestry is Taíno and Lucayan
My ancestry is sugar and rum
Everything nice and not so nice
My ancestry is the African Slave Trade
My ancestry is the British in India
My ancestry is coolie ships
My ancestry is an eighteen-hundreds village
Somewhere somewhere

Praise Be

*

Shrove Tuesday
        parade-of-the-bands
finds you begrudging
        a garden of snow

marrow in the
        "in between"

I solemnly declare
        to aspire

        to achieve

old calypso's irony
cum dissent, each note
of that now-distant pan
each trill, remains a calling
a pulse, a thrill

        index fingers to leaden sky
        shoulder to shoulder
        drum-chants, streets aquiver
        thousands of feet italicize

        Powah Powah

*

beside birch and sumac
despite dogwood
and black spruce
salted veins pulse
oceanwards
the sailor's phantom straw
a limb of pomerac

love-letter-cum-apologia
where no caimans bask
no pan-man 9–5 beats a tune
roti shop comparisons
> *who offers the most "authentic"*
> *curried duck?*

*

as leatherbacks to North Coast water
so to the merciless Southern Cross

you're back home when...

                           ...a tourist when

*

umbilical cords

     of bake and shark, pastel, tulum
     pig foot souse, pone, salt prune
     bus up shut, jeera pork, oil down
     Charlie's black pudding

severed
like a lizard's tail
grow back

My Heart, That Island

Chimera tropic, where
Shackle and cutlass

Manacle the mind
Beggar the begging

You differ with Quebec:
To re-member you must forget

J'ouvert morning's street thunder
My silvery love's kiss, her eyes

Hills orhanied in poui-pinks
Peekoplats put out on porches

Armoured emerita scamper to the sea
6 pm, scarlet ibis gash the sky

In the square the brilliant pianist
Sleeps beside Mahatma

My brother, sister, how will they find you?
Recruited? Hungry? Alive?

On Canada's stretched white canvas
Re-membering is colour

Terminus Temporary

I'd like to have known my very first parents—

No, not the recent kala pani—crossing
      Samdia, Dipraj, Samarsingh, Mathura, Bulaki, et al—
Or their forebears: the nameless South, and Broadly East Asians
Not the 16th and 17th century charioteers
(Who apparently hail from
Japan, Yakutia, and Mongolia)

> Nomad-me, I roam, then, honestly
> Generational powers—and defects—
> realized and unrealized, are harboured here
>
> Can one assign credit/blame?

Nor the one that renders me 0.4% Native American
Or the 4-percenter from the Neander Valley

> Btw, was it from you
> honorable 4-percenter
> I inherited my love of plants?
> Has your temerity been passed
> down? Will we survive the
> coming ice?

—No, no, no, not the heaving, thumper
Contract-expand-contract Amoeba

Rather

        To the indefinite nebulous beyond

    The can-only-be-fx-ed-to-be-imagined
    Impenetrable darkness
    Of time on the other side of time

The very very very first

      !Kaboom!

18

Fourteen billion years, and counting

Pre-primordial, the unhelixed one

Q: How loud that
how long that
!Kaboom!?

A: Well, it was "actually" a hummer, something like:
aaaa (*ad infinitum*)
uuuu (*ad infinitum*)
mmmm (*ad infinitum*)

How far backbackbackbackback
can you heeeeaaaar?

Mica, mica, parva stella
Luminous spheroids, rent asunder
Into themselves their centres sucked
Expelling expansion, expanding expulsion
The origins of you and me
In the crucible of nuclear reaction
Gold, silver, uranium
Masses and charges

Quirky quarks
Proton, electron, neutron
Hydrogen, carbon, nitrogen, oxygen
Miror quaenam sis tam bella

Specific antecedent
Energetic, violent
Particles of foremother

Atomos

How small small small small small can you go go go?

Precise enough
To presage

!Moi!

~~~~~

I would like, like gods amazeable —

Brahma, Vishnu, Shiva
creator, protector, destroyer
of the whole shebang

—to have witnessed
The time-taking, logic-making
Of seven octillion *Aha*s!

You who know it all
Have you been moved to admiration?
What astonishes *you*?

Domino-ing down evolution's parenting hwys
Celestial sequins diamonding
Segues gyral, non-sequence, and con-sequence
Rungs mundane, yet reliable as night parenthesizing day
To: *ta da!*

This here five-foot-four
Semblance traceable

Definitely, those eyes
those are the eyes
eyes of an atom

To primogenitor honorable

Atom-san

~~~~~

7 octillion Atom-sans + matter from exploding stars + a whole bunch of energy
× millions of millennia of the same + the 4-percenter from the Neander Valley
+ the 0.4% Native American + my ancestors who hail from Japan, Yakutia, and
Mongolia + the unnameable South, and Broadly East Asians + Samdia, Dipraj,
Samarsingh, Mathuras, Bulaki, et al + my more recent great-great-grandparents,
great-grandparents, grandparents, and my mother and father = the particular
me-ness of Me

I, Big Bang direct descendant
(lippy lips of an atom)
am (however)
childless

Bringing this fourteen-billion-year-old journey-adventure to

Psssst: Not So Fast

From *!Kaboom!* to this here five-foot-four
An accounting

The building blocks are

                                                    they just are

In the marrow of imagination
Infinity's duration weighed
Kalpa-synonymous, supereon-ymous
Endpoint-I's very own Bang
Essence of I, flotsam, and jetsam
Floats—or maybe blazes—through *ab immemorabili*
                          to the far side
                               of
                            eternity
Come Bulaki, come Samdia, Dipraj come, come Mathura
Come all ye indentured
Vivimus in aeternum
We ride the plume of the universe's drawn-out exhalation
Our saddle, fulcrum of time equidistant
Now is the hour of our future, now
                          Our dark and distant hum
Childless-I permeates   every thin film of every Planck
Ego in perpetuum vivum

                          I hereby bequeath percentages of me
                          to nieces and nephews waiting to be born

What is known
What is not known

Endless

Praise Be

"Bobby Shafto," "Blow the Wind Southerly"
"Oranges and Lemons," *Le Déjeuner sur l'herbe,*
"How sweet I roam'd from field to field"
"I wandered lonely as a cloud"
"The Tyger," "The Lamb"
The Hay Wain, The Boyhood of Raleigh
"The Little Black Boy," *The Blue Boy, Master Lambton*
The Vase with Fifteen Sunflowers, Wheatfield with Crows
A Sunday on La Grande Jatte
"Ode to a Nightingale," "The Eve of St. Agnes"
Great Expectations, Pride and Prejudice
"Tintern Abbey," "The Rime of the Ancient Mariner"
To the Lighthouse, The Waves, Orlando

These wings, my whistle's steel
This thundering heart
Forged in the oily fires of
Michael Anthony, Edwin Hing Wan
Ken Crichlow, Christopher Cozier, George Bailey
Paul Keens-Douglas, Hugh Stollmeyer
Abigail Hadeed, V.S. Naipaul, Shiva Naipaul
André Tanker, Samuel Selvon, Wendy Nanan
Edmund Hart, Harold Sonny Ladoo, M. Jacqui Alexander
Sybil Atteck, C. L. R. James, Lord Kitchener
Yao Ramesar, Meiling, Isaiah James Boodhoo
LeRoy Clarke, Kenneth Ramchand, Amy Leong Pang
Peter Minshall, Richard Fung, Kavir Mootoo
Patricia Mohammed, Ramabai Espinet, Banyan, Willi Chen...

Master Class

i
Dear Audrey, once handsome
Gentlewoman physician
Sits straight as a pin, draws her knife and fork in
Words pearl from her noble lips:

"The British"
                        Each mot a crystal pendalogue clinking
"Were
The best thing
Ever
To have happened

To India

Before *our* arr iiii val
India
You see
Had
No

Culture"

Colonizers, inheritors—present-day countrymen
For argument's intent let's suppose it's karma
That caused/allowed *you*
                        and not me
To, in effect, be conqueror, colonizer, benefactor—

Yes, yes, not *you* personally
but you who, on that side, reside
and, well, you know

benefit—

Your (for argument's sake) karmic (for argument's sake) destiny
To unapologetically manifest
Brawn, to rule, engage
In land-theft, occupation, resource robbery
The capture/enslavement of peoples
Families that don't reflect you—
Chits on game boards, sold piecemeal—
Millennia-old cultures shred to threads
The creation/dispensation of laws, rules—
Vocabulary of division and control—

Enormously monstrous atrociously heinous outrageously flagrant
Plunderer—
Offspring of Plunderer
It was you
Who inherited the earth

ii

What gravy still simmers in the perquisites of ordained skin? What
spoils of arrogance?

iii

Now, let's go along with this thing, karma

For argument's sake

It must follow that I, on the receiving end—
Karmically subaltern—
Opened the door

If when you see me you see only what you want to see, or
Try as you might (or not) you can't, for the life of you, consider me
It *has to* follow, then, that all socio-political inequities
Inflicted by you, yours, and your systems
On me and mine

are my own damn fault

As such, having no claims, I must release blameless you

But apparently, you don't exactly go scot-free

My Buddhist cohorts advise I need worry only about me
for, even as I tap my feet
the universe—ah, careful now dear Dear Audrey—is *taking care*

of you

iv
Alluring Audrey

Will I one day inherit you?
The law of entropy suggests random possibilities—
the random reorientation of you
your plundering karmic baggage
which I—
my heartfelt apologies—
had randomly suffered you
to drag around
the random reorientation of me
ah, your (admittedly) seductive
knife-edged arrogance—
who and what might I become?

I must train, refrain, restrain, say *NO*
To imitation

But what if we meet again? In some reoriented universe?

I must
One day
Sometime
Sometime in the near future
Wean myself
Off the opiates of vengeance

v
Dear Audrey,
~~It gives me great~~

Dear Audrey,
~~I have been~~

Dear Audrey,
~~You have been~~

Dear Audrey,

In through the nose
one two three four
out through the mouth, whoosh
one two three four five six seven eight
In through the nose
one two three four
out through the mouth, whoosh
one two three four five six seven eight
In through the nose
one two three four
out through the mouth, whoosh
one two three four five six seven eight
In through the nose
one two three four
out through the mouth, whoosh
one two three four five six seven eight

~~Dear Audrey~~

Inglan: A Green and Pleasant Land

the brown man's quotidian is rich
with neverthelesses

there is no mapepire
coiled
no scrunched-up doubles brown bag
discarded
beneath the wrought iron bench
set just so
amidst tended lawns and topiary
you sit, just so
composing lines in a book

the sleepy beauty of a weeping
willow
sun-rippled pond, preening swan
there's even a fountain
—it gurgles, too
in your village green
named after king and queen
human cargo transporter
plantation slave trader slave owner
country-carver-upper

Victoria Park, Regent's Park, Cassland Road Gardens
Colston Hall, Grenfell Park Road, Gladstone Park
Colston Girls' School, Colston Tower, the (tasty) Colston bun
Alston Road, Geffrye Museum, Thomas Picton *(Blood-Stained Governor*
(1797–1803) a.k.a. Tyrant of ((y)our) Trinidad has throughout the
"Commonwealth" roads, cities, pubs, and community centres
named after him)

immigrant sugar-and-spice child
you are a forever visitor
whose nevertheless-prerogative it is to wander
through every city nook and country cranny
of *This precious stone set in the silver sea*

(in the Lake District you strutted
as if you were Wordsworth himself
and recited lines from "Tintern Abbey")

~~~~~

monuments ubiquitous, marble plinths, gilded bronze
the winged victory stands upon a globe
the monarch wields her sovereign wand
victory wreaths, a *globus cruciger*
she points out to sea, *that over there, bring it to me!*
from one side of the mouth
vocabulary, syntax, grammar
amount always to the same cheer
to the English! to the English!

from the other side of the imperial mouth
dribbled on the likes of you
English dominance is over
        you

bronzed lions, naked youth, flaming torch
empire's heroes tower on stone horses, they watch
you come, and wonder when you'll go

how dare that brownie?
a recalcitrant child
who does not, cannot
know   how to be
          a grown man
—the brownie
in general, is no
freedom fighter
poet, nationalist
politician, teacher, activist

one need stretch little to understand
why you left backhome. but there? how come?

some went New York, some reach Toronto, some Miami
the question is therefore begged: of what fibre
what constitution he/she/they who picked
the break-and-enter nation, that trampled
our ancestors, plundered national treasures
drained the once-affluent subcontinent
of forty-five trillion dollars *forty-five trillion dollars*
forced citizens in the middle
of a blackout night *of a blackout night*
to get on their knees and crawl through streets
to get on their knees and crawl through streets
flooded communities, caused famine after famine
abetted kidnapping, conned the unguarded

into black-water crossing, committed mass murder
committed mass murder committed mass murder
did you imagine the land of the conqueror
would fling wide its arms, a welcome with choice
apologies steeped with blessings and sugar?
did you think they'd put a bandage on the past, and gild your future

every brown man
        cautions all that bronze, marble, and stone
harbours thanklessness, ignorance, and revenge

        to wit, he is
        a terrorist

who must, warns stone, forever be

        anesthetized
        pacified
        civilized

~~~~~~

oh, but how svelte you thought yourself
how chic, au courant
when you bought that second
television
an above-ground pool
the stand-up freezer

to garden party standards you mowed
and trimmed your iota
bordered it with hollyhocks and bunting
dianthus, delphiniums, peonies, and phlox
"In England's green and pleasant land"
your fantasized self, perfected in proximity to power

travels the Canaries, Naxos, Azores   wherever
on holiday shoulder-brushing empire's inheritors
armies of Raleighs
Drakes, Burtons, Livingstons
your new blue Brexit passport
and the globe between your teeth
Instagramming with your iPhone
every yacht, plate of pella de gofio
lemon roasted lamb, chicharros, and Cozido das Furnas

~~~~~~

caught out abroad, leg before wicket, a slap of the thigh
high-five and you admit
          you're Caribbean
      (*ha! they knew you'd get there in the end, you're Caribbean!*)

        yes, yes, make no mistake (you insist)—
          in the end—you are (insist, insist)

well, everywhere but in Britain—
             a Brit

~~~~~~

the tick that sucks the brain
what you would not admit you'd give
for a glimpse, just a glimpse
the surprise of her (oh, how she makes you forget
        the likes of Dyer and Lugard)
or him, either will do, behind the wheel
hey, corgis on the grounds will suffice
or the parting of a curtain
        an offspring
        husband or wife of offspring
        the cousin in a pinch, wife of the cousin
        a lady-in-waiting
        (you'd recognize them all)
        anyone, in fact, who across their body wears the sash:

            "One Hundred and Seventy-Eight Countries
                Invaded and Captured
            Seven Hundred Million Subjects Colonized
                    in Just
                Two Hundred Years"

child of empire
you star in each of those clauses

Brief Accounts of
the Brown Girl in the Ring
(tra la la la la)

Brown Girl in the Ring

Two-timer I am, infatuated
With the country in which I love
Yet yearning always for the one I left behind

***

I scratch my head until
Inner sores weep
For a theory
A tyranny of verbs
That might, just might, elucidate
The ubiquitous will
To drive a stake, conquer
Punish, enslave
Subjugate

Others, who
Like oneself, save
For the superficial of skin
Or tongue

love, eat, shit, make love, have sex, fornicate, grieve, sew, sing,
innovate, run, play, work, domesticate, plough, plant, pray, dream,
hate, suppose, connive, imagine, wish, hope, gossip, joke, debate,
relax, laugh, wonder, discipline, punish, judge, forgive, give, take, bleed,
cry, record, draw, paint, corroborate, cooperate, reward, suffer
jealousy, tell stories, lie, cheat, tell truth, punctuate, make symbols,
covet, celebrate, multiply, abstract, trade, analyze, believe, deceive,
kill, write, plead, medicate, dispose of the dead, invent, speculate,
build, tear down, rebuild, know Better, Never, Always, Right and Wrong

***

Contradictions are kindling:

If not for
Cristoforo Cristóbal Christopher
If not for George III and Victoria
If not for Isabel

                                    the fanatic

Would I even be?

Points of convergence
Karmically, cosmically
Conquerors, subjugators
Scavengers, opportunists
And
        bearing the burden strategically
Me

***

Guided by Toscanelli's *Atlantic Ocean 1474*
A Genoese seaman conjectures westward
                        from the backwater port of Palos de la Frontera
Divining Black Pepper and Marco Polo's land
Where roofs are sheathed in gold

Where he landed is still contested
        Turks and Caicos wrestles for the byline in tourism literature
                oh, to have been "Columbus's first"

                    moonstruck, dupable

sheeple we are
dazzled by rank
last, first, honours, percentages, caste

members of royal families
seldom buy their own drinks
sheeple, sheeple we

Cristoforo fancies arrival on Signor Polo's "the noble island of Cipangu"
a.k.a. Japan

or would that have been Java
or the Philippines?
These semi-naked supposed "Japanese" (Javanese, Filipinos?) did not
  speak
but gibberish, nor did these "Japanese" (Javanese, Filipinos?) know
of the Father, Son, and Holy Ghost

Land. Infidels. A land of infidels
A land of infidels and infidels on that land

Belong ~~Clearly~~ to no one

Up-for-grabs meets divine endowment's mandate
To sacrifice in Christian toil
The saving of infidel souls—
            i.e., to civilize

                              backwater-style
To civilize is to convert
            By coercion (if necessary)
i.e., to enslave, conquer, occupy, possess (if necessary)
                              backwater-style

41

So that they can be saved and know the One True Faith
God of the Catholics

in 1493 Pope Alexander VI—Rodrigo Borgia—
marvellously portrayed by Jeremy Irons in the 2011 TV show *The Borgias*
granted to the rulers of Spain
all the world not owned by Christians
so the heathens therein might be taught
he said, to embrace the Catholic faith
and be trained in good morals

backwater-style

***

The Genoese stabs the ground
In wound number one, he plants a wooden cross
Stabs again, and a standard fixed declares for Spain

The Genoese reads in Spanish to these notJapanese-Japanese
a proclamation claiming this notJapan-Japan
the Taíno island of Guanahani
for Spain
He renames Guanahani-Cipangu *San Salvador*
and encountering no resistance to his strange tongue
Colon pockets Guanahani San Salvador Bahamas Turks Caicos
as if they were cast aside on a crowded street, gold maravedi
he surreptitiously picked up, blew the muck off
and slipped in his pouch

a very nice side-hanging leather pouch, natural/fawn
falls on the hip, not too low, with weather protective flap
as seen in Royal Doulton's figurine
of this great explorer, created to honor the 500th anniversary of the

A likkle world with humanish critters who, btw, call themselves Lucayans
He thinks of no longer as Japanese but Indios
Captures seizes kidnaps imprisons a handful to include in his
cornucopia of other exotica
tobacco, pumpkin, avocado
pineapple, peanut, bell pepper
papaya, squash, corn, tomato
vanilla, turkey, potato
zucchini, cashew, cassava

Months later, Colombo lands on the island of Ayiti/Quisqueya/Bohio
which he believes is Cathay, a.k.a. China. He repeats the thrill of the
first crime, yanking the land, like a magic carpet, out from under the
feet of its inhabitants the Chinese who were really Taíno. He scratches
out Cathay, writes La Española, claims it and all the supposed Chinese
for Spain.
Oh Xi!

To Claim:
to state or assert that something is the case
typically without providing proof or evidence

which makes it sound as if the Taíno people
throughout the Caribbean
had been wilting forever on their beaches
staring eastwards to Spain, hoping if not praying

I imagine the Taíno whom the Genoese explorer encountered

loved, ate, shat, made love, had sex, fornicated, grieved, sewed, sang, innovated, ran, played, worked, domesticated, ploughed, planted, prayed, dreamed, hated, supposed, connived, imagined, wished, hoped, gossiped, joked, debated, relaxed, laughed, wondered, disciplined, punished, judged, forgave, gave, took, bled, cried, recorded, drew, painted, corroborated, cooperated, rewarded, suffered jealousy, told stories, lied, cheated, told the truth, punctuated, made symbols, coveted, celebrated, multiplied, abstracted, traded, analyzed, believed, deceived, killed, wrote, pleaded, medicated, disposed of their dead, invented, speculated, built, tore down, rebuilt, knew Better, Never, Always, Right and Wrong

***

Cristoforo, in his diario, wrote of the Taíno:

They traded with us and gave us everything they had, with good will... Your Highness can believe that in all the world there can be no better people. They love their neighbours as themselves, and they have the sweetest talk in the world, and are gentle and always laughing

***

I did not, first, wish to hurt you
Like mine your eyes, lips, breath
God, my noble intent
One True Faith
My Sword, your labour
Brandish my power

44

Your honeyed blood flows ruby
Dominion
Crushes guts sunders
Severs
Your head, dismembers
Your hand, your hands, your foot, your feet
What once was yours, your clan's
Is mine ours ours mine
Ecstasy
Of purpose, intent
Of reason
Erotic violent
Elixir transcendent
Sorrow prurient
I had to
I am sorry
Carnal
Forgive me
I had to

***

Backwater settlers enslaved
Bagged and sold by the "herd"
The In-all-the-world-there-was-no-better
And massacred the resistance

The entire labour force on Ayiti/Quisqueya/Bohio dead and gone
Backwater settlers headed backwater-style to Guanahani
And dragged *all* the Lucayan Taínos over to
Ayiti/Quisqueya/Bohio

Oh, islands in the sun

applause applause applause

Your forests, waters, your shining sands

applause applause applause

***

I beg you, do not get *marooned*
Get out of that *canoe* before the *hurricane* arrives
Store it in the *mangrove*, but watch out for *caiman*
Lie in the *hammock* while I empty your bag of *cassava*
And prepare for you that nice fat *iguana*, and all that *maize*
Go on, indulge in a little *tobacco*
While, this *turkey*, I *barbeque* for you

***

Was Cristoforo -topher -tóbal
ItalianItalianItalian? Church bells on a Sunday morning?

Were the backwater settlers
Reliably truly authentically certifiably entirely
(781 years of Muslim rule)
Old Christian?
Surely they were blushed
With the blood
Of Basque, Jew, and/or Moor

the main ingredient of Paella is what?
from where did it come?
and what about baqaayya?
go ahead, look it up

the will to invade conquer subjugate
exploit and extract
titillates, the undisciplined
trembling, hand in his pants, lurking

***

Not *every single one*:

Human nature
Being what it is

Borne out, or not entirely borne out
In mitochondrial DNA
Borne out, or not entirely borne out
In a portmanteau
Of Neverthelesses

Taíno and Lucayan live among us today

Bartolomé

Landowner-planter, raider, Indian slave owner
Cum preacher, political thinker, Dominican friar

OP, *Ordinis Praedicatorum*

Cum *encomienda* slayer
An ordinary man with—
what should not have been but was—
An extraordinary epiphany
Bartolomé chooses the dignity of the Native man

for they too, like him, he could see
loved, ate, shat, grieved, bled, cried, etc., etc.
Over personal gain, and returns
His Indigenous serfs to the governor

black friar

Bishop of conscience, race warrior
Court juggler of political and economic wills
And the ills of Indigenous slave labour
Bartolomé denies absolution
To Taíno slave owners

Dominican, *Domini canes*

In tract and letter
He whips with his pen

A Brief Account of the Destruction of the Indies Or, a faithful
NARRATIVE OF THE Horrid and Unexampled Massacres, Butcheries,
and all manner of Cruelties, that Hell and Malice could invent,
committed by the popish Spanish Party on the inhabitants of West-India,
TOGETHER With the Devastations of several Kingdoms in America by
Fire and Sword, for the space of Forty and Two Years, from the time of
its first Discovery by them
By Bartolomé de las Casas

Petitioning Castile and Aragon's Crown
Philosophizing, informing, debating
Theories of colonization and Christianizing
Morality, ethics, and spiritual well-being
The justness, the meaning of "Just War"

                                                    hound of God

He pleads the humanity of natives
Proposes intermarriage and equality of social integration
And in no uncertain terms condemns
As butchery and inhumanity
The Crown's Christian conquerors

                                            dog of the Lord
                                    "Protector of the Indians"

                        His Cause for Canonization
                            Is currently open

Intellectual architect of New Spain
God's masterful
Dignity-of-the-human
Saviour-of-the-Indian
Chess-player

Wrestles mortal facts of politics and economy
Nation-building and industry

            But who, who, if not for the Indigenous slave labourer
                                                so violently
                                            so abhorrently
                                                depleted
            Will perform the back-breaking of agriculture and mining?

Thinking thinking thinking
(No complaint for this curé without ample antidote)
What to do, what to do
How to save the Native, yet not slow
Spain's burgeoning fame and bloom

Et voilà! He earns himself a new distinction

Advocate for African Slave labour

Of people who

loved, ate, shat, made love, had sex, fornicated, grieved, sewed, sang,
innovated, ran, played, worked, domesticated, ploughed, planted,
prayed, dreamed, hated, supposed, connived, imagined, wished,
hoped, gossiped, joked, debated, relaxed, laughed, wondered,
disciplined, punished, judged, forgave, gave, took, bled, cried,
recorded, drew, painted, corroborated, cooperated, rewarded, suffered
jealousy, told stories, lied, cheated, told the truth, punctuated, made
symbols, coveted, celebrated, multiplied, abstracted, traded, analysed,
believed, deceived, killed, wrote, pleaded, medicated, disposed of
their dead, invented, speculated, built, tore down, rebuilt, knew Better,
Never, Always, Right and Wrong

it is said that in the Atlantic
sharks adjusted their migration routes
to accompany slave ships

Copious texts laud the Protector of the Indians

Fewer wrestle with his early advocacy of African slavery

50

How he parsed
From a Christian POV
Into what narrow crack
Falls a person
To render them enslavable?
Muslim, convert, "infidel"?
And from which region?
Senegal, Gambia, Mali
Angola, Congo, Gabon?
And which European nations
Can and cannot
Will and will not, might and might not
On the Middle Passage across the Atlantic
Transport human cargo

"Ergo" is a loaded notion
Cousin to "nevertheless"

12 million
Shackled
Tortured
Dead

NB
The Black Friar
In the waning of life
Hound of God
Sees light, and begs

                                              too too too way too late
                                           for profitability is a drug
                                     more basal than faith, hope, or love
                                            and the greatest of these
                                                         is love
                                           of self, gold, and power

Cajoles, shames
The Spanish Crown
To end enslavement

In matters of mass murder
Or less inflammatory, a large number of people dying, unnaturally, at
the hands of other humans

                              present day jurors, our own humanity at risk
                                       we wrestle with Las Casas
                                              juggle our own
                                       after-the-fact culpability
                                     as Intellectual accomplice
                                           "ergo" perpetrator
                                            "ergo" monster

S.O.S. from the underworld
Of No Return

Let us commemorate the finish line

                                          ends justifying means

Of a Christian journey
With a little Canonization, yes? A toast, a toast, to Las Casas
Hip hip

Resurrection

in the hands of the laity

Who do we think we are?

Resurrection

in the hands of the clergy

We know who they think they are

cui bono

But, hey, where are *they*? What are *their* names?

Who might *they*, had they

What could *they*, had they

Where would *they*, had they

The Meek inherit nothing

Contradictions are killing

Islanders hawk tourist candy of hibiscus and hummingbird
Silhouetting sunsets, people of colour making your bed

We whose enslaved ≠ indentured ancestors begat us
Distract and self-soothe, take pride in eating fire

Quickness coats our tongues
We chase all manner of fire with ron y coca cola, a cutlass

Scotch, and coconut water
(it good fuh yuh dawtah)

We have to
We have to

Fight and cuss and think we invented everything
Jump up, wine up yuh bumbum, be food-obsessed, sugar in any form

To live in an entire region founded on insane cruelty
It is reasonable to stare into the sun

And lick the belt that lashed our ancestors
That scars us now

So as not to go mad
It is reasonable to press your ear to steel and pan

To the millions of moaning ghosts
Of Indigenous people cut

From these, their Caribbean isles
How does bloody water look so turquoise

How does land that cradles the bones of people
So heartlessly destroyed by millions continue

To so profusely insist on life, as if each flower and bird
Were a breath come to life?

For them de las Casas gave his life's work, and yet...

If it weren't for old Bartolomé's introduction

Of the notion of the importation of African enslaved labour
Which, once served up to court

(Like a most tempting platter of albóndigas a la trufa)
(Prepared by, say, Ferran Adrià—if he'd lived back then, that is)—

Was bound to forever nag and excite every current or future greedy
  colonizer
The world—imagine this—might have had a chance, if only slight

To have been saved
Five hundred years

Of this particular iteration
        five hundred years
        and counting
Of the perpetual human problem
Of the unconscionable settler mind

Of racisms, abuses, injustices, and
            All manner of Cruelties, that Hell and Malice
            could invent

but in truth, might we have been spared
the silent revenge?
sugar
tranquilizing
everything
sugar in toothpaste
sugar in fruit juice
sugar in baby food
sugar in body soap
etc., etc., etc.

the usually prejudicial nature of diabetes?

Step up, or steups up
Who will
And who will not

Is this or is this not
Pause or Clause
For Canonization
Of Fray Bartolomé de las Casas?

Otherwise, would I even have come to be?
Catedrática, Catedrática
When you ask after my indentured ancestry
You're talking blood
When I answer, I, too, am talking blood

Not blood that flows in veins
But, wrought by Britain, France, Holland, Portugal, and Spain
That paid my passage here
And now floods the heart, the eyes, and brain

And yet
I am infatuated with
This country in which I love
Yearning, still and naturally
For the Island I grew up in

Ancestry not in the veins

The Big Despite

Couldn't quell the brilliance of resilience and resistance

Shivanee Ramlochan, Ingrid Persaud, Nikki Minaj, Vahni Capildeo
Eric Williams, Stokely Carmichael
Carlisle Chang, Hasely Crawford, Brian Lara
Winifred Atwell, Wendell Mottley
Dionne Brand, Wilmouth Houdini, Earl Lovelace
Adrian Cola Rienzi (born Krishna Deonarine), Patrick Manning
Chandar Bahadoor Mathura, Surujpat Mathura
Samuel Walrond, Sharon Mottley, Jean Pierre
A. N. R. Robinson, Rosa Guy
David Rudder, André Tanker, Winston "Spree" Simon
Ato Boldon, Beryl McBurnie, Hazel Ward
Boscoe Holder, Geoffrey Holder, Sir Lancelot
Attila The Hun, Roaring Lion, Colin Robinson, Rubadiri Victor
Uriah Buzz Butler, Michael Anthony
Cyrus Sylvester, Lord Melody, Errol Fabien, Drupatee Ramgoonai
Machel Montano, Audrey Jeffers, Ian Williams
Elizabeth Nunez, Errol Hill, Carlyle Kangaloo
The Mighty Sparrow, André Alexis
Derek Walcott, Pat Bishop, Lloyd Best
Romesh Dipraj Kumar Mootoo, Christine Kangaloo
Winston Dookeran, Karl Hudson-Phillips
M. NourbeSe Philip, Eintou Pearl Springer
Lisa Allen-Agostini, Calypso Rose
Keshorn Walcott, Robert Young
Kes 3 Canal, M. P. Alladin, Wayne Berkeley
Kathryn Chan, Claire Prieto, Basdeo Panday, Roger McTair
David Chariandy, Sahadeo Tiwari

to name but a few

Piper Nigrum/Black Pepper

Cook's Illustrated's testers assert
Is best ground fresh from the whole cherry
Native to Kerala's Malabar Coast
Found stuffed in the nostrils of Rameses II
Prized in old Rome as bribe and currency
Star ingredient in Asia's cuisines
Middle Ages luxury spice
   Of European aristocracy
Pretext for the Old World's pursuit of sea routes

To India, to India
To "seek Christians and spices"
And, centuries later
Back again, back again
For the labourer—
   Not of now out-moded black pepper, but
For the newer rum and Queen Sugar

If not for 19th Century Britain's role
CEO in its own clearing house
[   ]
   Senegal to Angola 13,000,000 humans
   (1500s, 1600s, 1700s, 1800s)
     The Bights of Benin and Biafra
     The land that laid the golden guinea (1663–1816)
     4,803,000 from there alone (1501–1867)

If not for Britain's 300-year-long
[   ]
   Commerce, Christianity, Civilization
   Boot on the neck

⅓ of the world
Destruction of life
    Of culture
    Identity theft
Dispersal of humans
    Seeds it hadn't imagined
        Would rise
            Rise up, rise up

If not for the brutish rule of India (1599–1947)
    From where they
[   ]
    3.5 million Indians (1845–1917)
    As if humans were blooms of iron ore
    Bricks of tea, barrels of salted cod

If not for La Isla de la Trinidad (1797)
[   ]
Would Indra and Romesh have found one another?

And I be scratching
History, sifting heaven's dust
For Ancestry?

Entanglements
    Accrued
        Accursed

The Nevertheless Queen

In musings of ancestry
La Católica, "pro" and "an" tagonist

Queen of lust for land
Greed for gold

Absolved from all
Papal Licences

Shielded by Doctrines
Of Discovery

Non-Christians do not have dominium over territory
Barbarous nations be overthrown
Their land discovered, claimed, subjugated
and

In a short while your hardships and endeavors will attain the most
felicitous result, to the happiness and glory of all Christendom

The first causality of colonization:
Colonizer

Crashed, shattered, spent
The death of one ocean's wave
Is another's conception

It turns out the question
Is not so much about means
As it is about ends

If not for you, self-styled
God-appointed saviour
Catholic Monarch, La Catolica

                                                    to some

                                                      .

                                                      .

                                                      .

                                                    fanatic
                                                    to others

Initiator of Europe's rise
        Like a Kraken
        Out of its backwater

This contested world might be in kinder hands

From where you sit now
Looking down

                                                    or is that *up*?

How does God's Servant sum it all up?

In His name
Your Inquisition

Your royal rabid decrees
Your expulsions, your mass death and suffering
Your forced conversions

2,000 living humans
Burned at your stakes

In His name
The actions of your fear of Jewish infidels

Bible-led banishments
Of people who for 1,500 years
Had inhabited their Iberian Peninsula

200,000 forced conversions
40,000 Jews expelled

Jewish-Muslim-Christian *Convivencia*
Set afire

Btw (1): as you watched your husband Ferdinand
Your son Juan
Daughter Isabella
Grandson Miguel
All sick and dying
Did you wish for Jewish doctors?
The ones you'd banished?

Is tantamount to hate

Bella
Your unshakeable certainty
Rock-hard in your faith and rule
That tolerance and acceptance are evil
Made a virtue of Christian Pride

Royal fanaticism and paranoia on steroids

In His name
Islamophobia

In your name
Islamophobia

> Btw (2): Granada was Iberia's treasure trove of silk
> Pearls and taffeta
> Dried fruit, nuts, and almonds

In the name of your Father, Son, and Holy Ghost
Your unholy kiss of the Iberian Peninsula:
Neighbour, turn against neighbour

> Did you see him change his shirt on Fridays?
> Did you see him eat the pork? But how?
> Did you witness him take pleasure in his eating?

In His name
To unify Spain
In His name
Your political gain:

> Looking down—or is that *up*
> What would you say, pious queen
> Did you, or did you not, call His name in vain

You and yours financed Genoese starboy's adventures
(Does it ever irk you that today he gets more press than you?
Do you think it's because you're a woman?
It's probably why in some versions Ferdinand, as King, eclipses you?)
Isa dear, maybe it's better this way;
You know, all those expulsions, your forced conversions
The Inquisition, the burnings
The centuries you spawned of
Caribbean poverty
Blood and killing
All in your (and His) name
It's heady stuff, let them take the blame
To circumvent the sophisticated wealthy
Infidel orient

Overland of Turk and Persian
And the Arabs who'd protected and translated
Greek philosophy and mythology
Wrote the first illustrated encyclopedia of surgery (approx. 1000 AD)
Created the first degree-granting university (859 AD)
Wrote and sang ghazals, developed the arabesque
Invented the magnifying glass
The camera obscura (around 1000 AD)
And most—absolutely most—importantly, gave the world the gift of coffee
And China with such a strange, but clever thing: paper money
Amongst many many many many many many
Many many many many many many other things
And lots more

Across thousands of miles of ocean blue
A bridge to the Carib Sea of blood
You enflamed Europe's lust for rule
God's Servant
New World and all of that
Lands defined as empty

∴ conquered legally

Infidels for the Christianizing
Christianized infidels for enslaving
Every resource ripped from the land
From Natives' hands
Consigned to Spain
For nothing in return

the ease with which one can crush a skull
hunger not in the belly
blinds the heart
makes truth of fantasy and fables
reason of illusions
zealots of hearsay
every jungle conceals an El Dorado
in suspension
awaiting your conquistador
walls, oh walls of gold
dishes, oh dishes of gold
hardware, oh stirrups of gold
roads and roads of gold
handfuls of ingots of gold
saddlebags of ingots of gold
boatloads of gold
gimme gimme gimme

                                        all your gold
                                torbellinos in the mind
                           blowflies lapping at the soul

                                   a nevertheless insistent
                                              or else
                       shackles reason and courts crushing skulls

                                          as many as necessary
But the building of palatial churches
And settler mansions

How could you, Servant mother
Pious Queen have done this to us?
                                        each wave spawns another
Your legacy to present-day us:
A psychological attachment
                        deeper than any mine in which "your" Taíno died
To oppression
                                    we've learned to oppress ourselves
                                           by oppressing others

Was it worth it?

Your New World, after 500 years, going out, crashing, shattering
(but I shouldn't be so harsh—you were just a Servant, not a seer)

Your rule
From the POV of this descendant
Of Indian Indentureship in a skin-deep
Beautiful but heart-sick Caribbean
Has, nevertheless

history
is a series of
"Nevertheless"

Turned out, indeed, to be
A case of means and ends

Nevertheless, a few would say

a few, a few

Justified   and justifies
Your rhyme and means:
Spain, united by the belt of Catholicism
All those statues of you
And your barbarous conquistadores
Columbus, Cortez, Juan de Oñate
Ponce de León

Which will stay standing today?
Which will come down?

The following cannot be a footnote:
Canonization by the Catholic Church
A process in 1970 that *"could be undertaken with a sense of security
since there was not found one single act, public or private, of Queen
Isabella that was not inspired by Christian and evangelical criteria;
moreover there was a 'reputation of sanctity' uninterrupted for five
centuries"*

In 1972   Isabella of Castile   was awarded the title
In this the first stage   in the process toward   sainthood
The title of "Servant of God"

Spain's Inquisition was not fully abolished until until until

Being Here

In a northern extension of the terracide
Begun by Popes, Queens, and Kings

I, too, have settled here

I came, I just came
It was easy
I could, so I did
And stayed, I just stayed
Roots were planted

I, too, had not asked, nor was permission granted
What is the weight of gratitude brandished
For what's not given, but rather, taken

Be it yesteryear, today, every day?

I close tight my eyes, cover my ears
And speak Nation names
Faster than a speeding bullet while I hope and just carry on

Acknowledge, acknowledge
But do not ask

I know whose land this is

I live on
Anishinaabeg land
Wendat land
Haudenosaunee land

Technicalities of "covered by Treaty…"
"Ceded" and "unceded"
Stated by whom and when
Legalities placate and underline
Omissions, pauses, fabricate, and mold
"History"

I acknowledge the magnificence, Mother, in this life-enriching, this
    aching, Land
I endeavor to be forever cognizant of my complicated good fortune
not as uninvited guest, not as an admitted settler mea culpa-ing
    nevertheless onward
but as one who stands in every way I can with Land's protectors,
    Water's protectors
with both hands, this mouth, lungs, mind, heart, and feet in the
    recognition of
in the struggle against, a through line of past, of contemporary
    injustices
against Land, her First inhabitants, all her descendants

In the Theatre of War
(or The Philosophizer's Popcorn)

Killed begs the question
Not of who was killed so much as
Who pulled that trigger?

Not a name
Sometimes a face

But this is too much
Like looking in a mirror

Rather, the essence of that Who

A clue to the confounding
Why?

Trees die, birds
Garden hose nozzles
Babies, stars, the car

Computers die, prophets, the czar
Queens, farmers, bees

Things fall apart—as good as die

Are circumstances really
Excusable, understandable, acceptable?

What is the meaning of *really*?

Of human? Killer? Accomplice?

Even when *how* is categorizable

Self-defence, compassionate, punishment
　　　All ways necessarily parse-able

One on one, one against two, or a few
Forging chasms in history
Nation building, expansion of borders

Because
Is as malleable as

I am God and God said so

Fieldwork of murder
Followers of orders
Fingerprint on the trigger

The Essence, the Marrow
Of every singular Who

No lesser no greater than
The signature on the order

And yet, and yet:

In the theatre of murder
The poem is an alibi
The philosophizer's popcorn
War makes an accomplice
Of the most horrified sideliner

Limbo
(yes, like me)

Matayla, Matayla

Your once-white too-big dress kept pace
Cinched at your meagre waist with rope
That could draw a bucket from a well
Tie a cow, the feet of a woman, hang a man, oneself
Upon your head gnats and storm clouds swirled
Mashed-up black shoes hastened you
A woman forsaken?
Vivified by some revolt
Or divination?
Clutching a black handbag
Like a pass, or it carried proof
Some legal document, a photograph?
Where did you go? The hospital?
Cemetery? To see a friend?
To sit on a bench at King's Wharf
Gaze out at the murky Gulf
Search for a ship you once knew?

Squatting on pale white gravel
You scrubbed, washed, scrubbed
Out of a rusted Klim tin
What might have been
Your only piece of underwear

The stragglers took aim with
Slingshots and guava sticks
Your screams incomprehensible
Water from the well of your milky eyes
Couldn't put out the fire

One to ten, and they came at you again

From where did you come?
Were you born on the island?
Did you come here running?
Were you dragged?

Did you know a man who went by the name of King Radio?
What about H. Belafonte?
Was it you who took their money and ran Venezuela?

Everyone called you Matayla. Is that even your name?

Sapodilla

If I anthropologize à la Proust
in *The Guermantes Way,* let me
not look for clues or claims to ancestry
in the shape of a nose, jawline, the lunge
to handshake, the tenor of a comment
delivered, preference for one kind of company
over another, but also, at methods
of showering. Is not the imprinting
of a roadside Black or Indian man
observed in childhood from the back seat
of an idling car, not as affecting as DNA?
In the privacy of my indoor shower, under
a fine hot spray, before my body—or
should that be society—began
its long journey of betrayals
I did as I saw and lathered my materiality
to dream-permitting insertions

*

Naked save for flag-red underpants
In the recessed pool
Of a countryside roadside standpipe
He stands, casual, dark-skinned body suds-streaked white
Each outstretched muscled arm he lathers steadily
Then raises his eyes to the sky where frigates swirl

His sinewy neck he swizzles to oceanic foam
Oblivious—perhaps accustomed—to curious eyes
He pivots, his back to roadside, hands—
Conceivably—inside skin-tight pants
He faces the road again, hands now behind him
Thighs and calves he nimbly soap-paste laminates

Each arched heel he scrubs, flamingo pink
Upright again, the lather-whitened man's fingers
Rise and fall, octopus-like on his head of resistant hair
Eyes closed, in a bloom of thick white cream, his face erased
From an overflowing bucket he draws a saucepan
Prismic bubbles river down his head, face, torso, limbs
Now glisten sapodilla-seed-brownness
The idling cars, this girl-child, studying
Have garnered not one iota of notice

Today, every time I take a shower, my cleansing heredity
In the lengthening distance my lathering echo
Fisherman-muscled, roadside-thin, standpipe-tall

When finally we rinse
The caked balm of white
Rainbow shards glisten
On wet sapodilla-skin

Documentary: Indian Limbo

Introduction

From 1845 to 1917 (cannot be a footnote) 143,939 Indians left India
    (cannot be a footnote)
for indentureship in Trinidad (cannot be a footnote). 90% did not return
    (cannot be a footnote)

> doctor lawyer madman boss
> Muslim Christian Brahmin Chamar
> fisherman taxi-driver market-seller prof
> businesswoman drug-dealer Trini-toff
> teacher preacher yardman nurse
> alcoholic drug-addict jeweller
> roadside-beggar mass-man pan-player
> president minister dancer artist writer

> how Indian is a little or a lot of Indian
> in the blood of an Indo-Trinidadian
> who, no matter where they reach
> is a Trini to the bone?

neverthelesses and *albeits* considered
turning around, squinting, looking back

Dookhoo
Bhola
Haitram
Askaran
Ankaroo
Gabdo
Kangalee

Kawal
Gangadin
Basant
Rushparr
Ramkishun

et al

restless man of adventure
young radical woman visionary
money-making opportunist

fugitive from farmlands lost
from famine and taxes
the British and their Zamindari

escapees
of plagues
of other hawan and taiga
of the sepoy mutinies
of inheritance inequality
of gender and sex discrimination
incarceration, unwed pregnancy
unwanted marriage arrangement

of annexations by the British—territory after territory

or just plain-old poor, powerless, prospectless
easily fooled tricked kidnapped trafficked
something unimagined, mis- or not understood

Trinidad is around the corner, says the arkatiya
go, one year, maybe two, work—cut cane
pick cacao, two three hours a day—no more
then sit under the shade of a chenette tree
suck chenette while you chinny chalay
you make so much money
try counting the grains of sand by the sea
then come home to India, and live like the boss

of course, you'll come back, we'll make very-very sure

would Dookhoo to Ramkishun et al
when they committed that most unholy act
        crossing water
have imagined Trini you and Trini me?

i.

1845
227 Girmitiyas
Men to women, 10 for every 4
Transported on the *Fath Al Razack*—
Victory of Allah the Provider

Tempting the mad sea
Of white-maned tides
To stake their chances

Blind

ii.

For 79 days
Roiled the pagal samundar
Caste-devouring kala pani

For 79 days
15 superficial feet was home

For 79 days
Their ship played roulette
With cholera

iii

On the 79th, May 30th, the gangplank lowered
A one-way bridge

        a line
        begun at recruitment
        underlined

A sandalled foot touches land

        the line builds
        a wall

227 migrants
Calligraphed
Minions exercise their curlicuing flourishes
                                       and phonetics
Registration number, name, father's name
                                       the power to name and misname
Sex, age, estate

                        another brick—

                        newly surnamed, a misspelled migrant
                        harbours in her heart of hearts
                        Hanuman, Saraswati, Buddha, Ganesh
                          Bibi Fatima

                        she knows who she is
                        hope is a chance
                        to become

                        —fortifies her wall

iv.

Bound to Bonne Aventure, Williamsville
Brechin Castle, Orange Grove, Reform
Woodford Lodge, Usine St. Madeleine

Working for
Tennant and Sons, R. J. Warren, Wilson, Pile
G. T. Fenwick, Gregor Turnbull, R. de Verteuil
S. Henderson, H. Cornilliac, John Cumming
Chancery, McClean, Mrs. Rowbottom, McIntosh
W.F. Burnley, Price Brothers, F. W. Le Blanc, et al

9-hour weekdays, five on Saturdays
A shilling a man a day
Nine pence a woman

+

4 chittaks of rice daily
2 chittaks of dhal daily
½ chittak of ghee daily
¼ chittak of salt daily

One blanket yearly
Two dhotis yearly
One chintz jacket yearly
One Lascars cap yearly
One wooden bowl yearly

one brass lota per four people

dig, plough, plant, cutlass, transport, weed, dig, plough, plant, cutlass,
   transport, weed, dig
dig, plough, plant, cutlass, transport, weed, dig, plough, plant, cutlass,
   transport, weed, dig
dig, plough, plant, cutlass, transport, weed, dig, plough, plant, cutlass,
   transport, weed, dig
dig, plough, plant, cutlass, transport, weed, dig, plough, plant, cutlass,
   transport, weed, dig
dig, plough, plant, cutlass, transport, weed, dig, plough, plant, cutlass,
   transport, weed, dig

long time, no time, a lifetime, who backhome has died, what niece or
nephew born, what songs have come and gone, who remembers me
will I taste her hand again, her face against mine, does anyone dream
of me, what shape the future, I hope, is the sun, are the stars, the moon
my name

Cracks in the wall

   Then | Now   There | Here   Past | Future   There | There
            Cry | Cry   Don't Cry | Look at the Camera

And another five

weed, cutlass, plant, plough, dig, save, weed, cutlass, plant, plough,
    dig, save, weed
weed, cutlass, plant, plough, dig, save, weed, cutlass, plant, plough,
    dig, save, weed
weed, cutlass, plant, plough, dig, save, weed, cutlass, plant, plough,
    dig, save, weed
weed, cutlass, plant, plough, dig, save, weed, cutlass, plant, plough,
    dig, save, weed
weed, cutlass, plant, plough, dig, save, weed, cutlass, plant, plough,
    dig, save, weed

Yes Sir, Yes Sir | Plenty Hogsheads Full

Cane, commerce, country, cultivated
Every year, every marriage, every child born
Every tree planted, bicycle bought
Body on the banks of the Caroni burned

Line underlined
Thickened to walls
And limbo poles

Under which bodies
In daytime contorted
Nighttime swayed
                    Pooja, cutlass, gamblers, school work, estate rum
Necessary oblivion

Conch shells blown were missives dispatched

v.

In cots of sugared glass
They dreamed
Generations of us   into being

The Beginning The End

Recruited, indentured, Bulaki's ship's baggage allowance would hardly
    have included
heirloomable furniture, or let's say his father's hand-carved peerha
    his great grandmother's notebook of dream-poems, portraits of
    ancestors, say, or say, a pair of porcelain terriers

Whatever he bore
From land to ship
From ship to land
To estate barrack
From estate barrack to estate barrack
To little home, from little home
To larger one

Was long ago discarded / lost—no inheritance from a pre-175-years-
ago backhome fantasy has consequently reached these open palms
in the 21st century. No legacy embroiders / reinforces our new-world
salty walls and beetled shelves, no lineage to instruct / inhibit Bulaki's
begetting

Rather, in the grab-and-go of this forefather, from that moribund empire
I inherited

The practice of leaving
Of forgetting
Of discarding

The storied scratched and worn

The latest fandangle traded for the next, the next, and the next
    momentarily trending trifle

Knocking on Bulaki's end point brick-wall of ancestry
We learned our lessons well:
      to rob ourselves of the skills of excavation and conservation
We laugh—as we must—mindless
      of tomorrow, of next year, of unborn eyes

We

We

Around the neck of a phantom future "we"
I wear the hand-me-down necklace-noose
of arrival

but hey, no landing

La catedrática from the publish-or-perish univers-ity
Picks irishbornindotrinidadianlesbiancanadianwriter me

Not just bone, but meat on bone
In this hierarchy of diners and dine-ees
La catedrática chews
On me

Marrow in the bones
Blink neon-red
Yet I of the nomad-epidermis
Keen for visibility

Peelpeelpeel

Willingly is a parsable notion

Held up to her lamp
In the grip of tenured tweezers
Poked and prodded
I wriggle

Then, I
Dancer for the patron

Twirltwirltwirl

Carnival Monday, midday heat
like a Robber
parched

who drifts

on the deck
of a ghostly ship

that never
docks

Scalp defleshed by her jester's thorny crown
her poetry-chant
muddled

From the moistened lips of la catedrática, a thesis hustled

Kala Pani

In the scratching of backs
will you ever-never learn
mutual is proportionate, if not contestable?

There are no records
No diaries, no photographs
No letters from Bulaki's "backhome"
No envelopes scripted in hinglish
No postcards, invoices, lists
No passed-down mangalsutra
Books with marked-up margins
Taria, lotah, conch shell, kara

Well, surely there are present-day scars, she insists?

Oh God, I must
to exist
whether or not
weather and knot
conform
to the coralitude of Torabully

Nod-nod, compliant-us, wink-wink, willing-me/we

I mine
other people's stories
to picture my own

meanwhile

No need for any foreign authority:
we fully capable
of colonizing oui!

Sentries among us scout the hole
For those of us who dream of climbing out

Individuality is a crown

not worn by the colonized

So, I press the ajees and ajahs
And get only *ohos* and *ahas*
That, in truth
What a shame
Come to think of it
No one in the family
Actually *no one*
Ever mentioned that longlonglong-ago sea

Sure, someone went back, but who wants to remember a returnee?

Basdei says, You know who you should ask? Ask Auntie Jess
Auntie Jess says, Ask Uncle Ramdin—he would surely know
Uncle Ramdin scratches his chin—
He doesn't know what nonsense Bas and Jess are talking about

But what about you, he asks, which mas camp you playing in this year?

I/"We" acquiesce, bundle myself/ourselves, tie the knot
Hum to the tune of the ready-already one-size origin song

Collaborators

                                        Hey, wey yuh go do?

Perpetuating the colonizers' tried and true
Existence guaranteed
En masse
In conformity

                                        Uniqueness, a privilege
                                        not granted the coolie

                                        I must must I
                                        speak her Euro-tongue
                                        to tantalize her
                                        curating me

They did this, they did that
We   Our   Our   We

My existence-insurer professor will surely lose interest
if I am all bones, no meat

Anthropologically-colonizing-her
native-informing-me

She manacles me

For the name of an estate, wages, a cutlass swinging
Slicing cane, a head, a hand in jealousy, drunkenness, despair

And btw, what does India, mother country, mean to me?

I tell her
skin
is a roguish thing

And toss about
Mathura, Capildeo, Jamadar
pre-'60s—the Trinidad independence movement
'70s—Black Power
anytime of any day or night—bobol at the highest levels of government
today—ocean pollution off the East coast, quarrying the Northern Range
and '64—Two White Women Travelling Through Africa (Africaaaa)
and next time she visits—make sure to see
the leatherback turtles that crossed her kala pani
to nest at Matura, Fishing Pond, and Grand Riviere

To exist, she advises
Regale us, rather, with tales of
Contemporary Indo-indenture despair
And the cut-out mother mother mother mother tongue

This nomadic victim-coolie-mangalsutra decorates
but does not liberate

The tongue, I respond, bleeds more profusely than any other part of the body

And reattachment of a tongue
is possible if done within 8 hours of its amputation

A delay of 8 decades or four generations can result in legends of complications

OK, OK, how about diabetes, guns, money, drugs

Gagnant, gagnant!

For there to have been a victim
a crime must have been committed

A crime *was* committed

What am I, wherever I go, if not somebody's

forever-victim

forever-coolie?

Great-great-grandfather, did you walk? how? with verve? were you running? from what? to what? at what speed? approximate for the sake of story—were you, for instance, panting? looking over your shoulder? help me to exist—tell stories, embellish with colour—reds and gold, did clothes get torn? talk to me even if I don't understand—and then so I understand, in hindi, bhojpuri, hinglish, whatever, just talk, pepper—or haldi, as you wish—your/my origin story with aromas, how about some recipes? hardships, hardships overcome, the cutlass—surely there was one, more than one? a gun? money borrowed, money lent? an arrangement you didn't like, an unsuitable girl, a boy with pink lips and twinkling eyes?

The colonized tutored, becomes the colonizer
the gaoled, the gaoler

Great-great-grandmother, what did you leave behind? who? had you
been indiscreet? what did you bring with you? a handful of earth? did
you cut locks of your hair and bury it back there? were you like me—you
know what I mean—they say it runs in families—were you desperate—
an adventurer, did you play cricket, or back then climb, or at least
approach, Mount Everest? oh say, say, say it is so! how about when you
got here—did you look at the poui-clad northern range and dream? did
you scribble poems, did you have a dog, a parrot, ride a horse? what
compromises did you make, great-great-grandmother, were there any
gains? would you have considered/would you have loved   me?

Is adventure-seeking—in an Indian—a symptom?

Did they grab you in the dark, drag you, you kicking
   screaming, terrified? did they trick you?
Did you suspect and still, perversely curious, go along?
If up shot your hand, did you flex your muscles
   in a show of labour-ability, *take me take me*?

If so then it is fair, is it not, to say *you left*? left willingly?

Is there a contemporary value to the notion of *willingly*?

Tell me stories—not for la catedrática, but for me

OK, OK, the turban started out white—

Yes, likely—
but why not also decorate it—say, with a jewel from the mother country

Well, OK, the Star of India

But it fell overboard in a fight, you see
that left a scar
that got passed down
genetically

Why didn't *you* return, great-great-grands?

What did you see/know/dream of/hope for that made you stay? did you imagine me?

How hard does one have to try to have tried hard?

Help me, great-great-grands, verify and demonstrate

The persistence and weight

Of *want*

My father has a plaque on his wall—
If a man wants his dreams to come true

Go ahead, finish it

My great-great-grandfather was truly great, I regale

When, within days of the start of the journey, the Star of India on his turban fell overboard, he stared up into the sky every night, scornful yet breathless, searching heaven's sequins for a sign. On the journey's first full moon, he saw the big white face blink, and without thinking, as if moved by the forces of heaven, he lassoed it with his suddenly lengthened and lengthening string of rudraksha beads. Caught in his mind's line, he flew the full moon across the Indian Ocean. Oh, how it spun in his hands round the Cape, and dipped, rolled, and rose high above the bumpy Atlantic highway, night after night guiding the ship in pearly moonshine. Clouds came out to see the phenomenon of the usually self-centred moon trailing my great-great-grandfather. Surprised, and in awe of the previously unknown, melting heart of this white moon, the clouds dared not insert themselves between this man and his moon. And only when the ship anchored in Port of Spain, did great-great-grandpa—hesitant, unsure of his place of abode—cut loose the moon— but the moon, having fallen in love with its gaoler, behaved like a lover misunderstood, spurned, reluctant to leave. It bobbed in the sky and for a fortnight cried a bloody aura.

It did eventually float away, though, across the brilliant ocean of Caribbean sky.

Pune and Delhi

Everyone resembled someone I knew
Relatives, friends, teachers, shopkeepers

I half-hoped for a quizzical stare, and
In the surprise of unexpected recognition
Someone runs up, throngs gathering, to declare:
"You, you are Samarsingh, yes?
We've been waiting, oh, no-no, never
We never gave up hope"

On the streets, in the shops, syllables scattered
Like broken rice
Rapid-fire as the wedding tabla

If I was being enlightened,
Take my hand, come home, come meet us all
Or told, *Go, go back to where you came from*
Unless they spoke my Trini grandmother's acha and chalo

Or Mrs. Balbir's Singh's *The Art of Indian Cookery*
Or "Taj Mahal," "Red Fort," Hare Rama Hare Krishna
Or Nat Geo's thousand-year-old caves in which Buddhas recline
I, great-granddaughter of Samarsingh
Wanting so furious-fast I appear to be standing still, can only
Wish throngs would concur that this, all of this, is mine

I'm told, rather, in perfect English
We in India were never in indenture
And reminded of my date of departure

Claims of belonging
Kala pani—damaged dreams

In an 1890s ship's registry
Silverfish-eaten entries
Long expired

Witness, Oh Witness Dey!

Witness, oh Witness dey

        History's whistle-blower's divine cause, pinpoint effect

Unmuzzle

If you see, then speak

When are transgressions not transgressions?

My brother, why can't you why can't you why won't you
Get that monkey off your back?

Neighbour-neighbour, jahaji cousin, it is always
You
Who finds him
Last week, by the library corner, you say, like a chicken scratching dirt
Last month, like a vagrant by the hospital gate begging alms
Just like that
You
Always find him
You
Take him for Subway and KFC, try your best to put sense in his head

You
Always
Bring him home

You tell my father he and you are jahaji cousins—
Your forefathers, you reminisce (as if unborn-you were there)
And my father's, jahaji bhais
Together huddled on the ship's deck

The kala pani, you lament

                                        Pinpoint cause, divine effect

Watched and washed us all
Into existence
This side of castelessness

In front my bending father you beseech my brother
He mustn't, you tell him, a tear in your eye
Really, he must and mustn't
In any case, it's all about who gets the money, you sigh
And, oh, what a good family he comes from, our ancestors, you say
Same ship, he should and shouldn't

This lost, grateful father, begging you to stay
Slowly pushes in the door as you leave
He would give you the shirt off his back

You say, Uncle, we are all jahaji relations
—It's the least I can do

The old man doesn't see that you've barely left his yard
And two-faced you, you're already texting orders
To other jahaji cousins:

—Shipment in this evening
Flood the streets by dawn

—Corner your corner

—Wait two days then deliver
Another round to the boy

—No, no, gun not necessary, the father, Indian-father-to-the-bone
always pays

2 4 6 8
Mootoo by the College Gate
Eating roti from a plate
2 4 6 8

Town-grown white boys shove skinny Indian
Tunapuna Indian, country-boy, roti-boy, to the ground
His lunch pail is a racatang football, kicked out his hand
Roti-roti, bread of the silent Indian
Dhal mop-upper of the coolie-class

White boys stick a ruler through the roti, raise it like a flag
And around the school yard race

2 4 6 8
Mootoo by the College Gate
Eating roti from a plate
2 4 6 8
Mootoo by the College Gate
Eating roti from a plate

Mootoo learns to crouch
In the empty classroom at lunchtime
He lifts the lid of the desk, and hides behind it
Devours, in two twos, Chachi's 5 am-cooked roti and talkari

Thames-side, London-Ontario, a park
(aflame in autumn reds)

Under the shade of a sugar maple
Witness departed my body
Stood off to the side and observed

Son of an Indian diplomat
                    A veritable Indian from India
            with whom I had fantasized authenticity

Stroked my thigh and corrected me:
The descendants of the Indians who left India in the 1800s as
Indentured labourers
Are not real Indians. You
                            He instructed, if not diplomatically
Are all bastardized Indians

With or without prejudice, Witness?

Back home—

        Oh where is this *backhome*, where oh where
        who is back and how is home?

(Trinidad) to celebrate the university's conference on Indian literature
dinner in the attendees' honour, held at the Port of Spain residence of
the Indian high commissioner

Wife of the high commissioner, saried and bejewelled, green eyes
averted—at her phone, to the loud-ticking wall clock—shoulders
pinched in, she slides through the roomful of hyphenated Indians of
who-knows-what castes—caste breakers, descendants of kala pani—
transgressors, university-cooped-up hopefuls trying their darndest to
excavate traces of Mother India
              the clock the door the clock the door
Trapped in what she will allow to be no more than a six-sentence
conversation, the finger of the wife of the Indian high commissioner
wags on the words *Never* and *We*: But *We* were *Never*, provoked by
some intellectual trying to be as Indian as she, *We* were *Never,* you see
Never, We were *Never* indentured, indentured labourers *Never* were *We*

                 A Witness must not be muzzled
                       Unscold the Witness

video recorder in my hand
the gun of it pointed at Lal
he juggles
a loaded hesitation
eagerness apologetic

I was four.
We were on the train, my mother, my father and me.
We had been travelling for many hours. We were on our way to see my
mother's parents in another state. I was hungry. We had fallen asleep.
The train stopped. We got out and my father bought chapatis from a
woman vendor. We were waiting to get back on board. Two men who
looked like my father, except they were dressed better than he, came
to us and began to chat. They asked where we came from, where we
were going, if we ever heard of the West Indies. We didn't know what
they were talking about. They offered to buy us food and drink. They
took us to a café by the train station and bought food for us and alcohol
for my mother and father. Suddenly my father, drunk now, realized the
train had gone and left us. The men told us not to worry, another train
will come, and they will look after us. We got on the other train with the
men. The men gave us all something to drink and told us they will wake
us up when we arrive. They seemed like nice men. When we woke up, we
were on a ship, already on the ocean, and we watched the land we were
leaving, never to return, far away, getting smaller in the distance.

We are famous

Lal laughs furtively

It was 1917, we came on the last ship to bring indentured labourers to
Trinidad, the S.S. Ganges. We are famous.

2 4 6 8

What do you know, Witness? Did Lal's father and my great-great-grandfather Bulaki speak? Did they vomit together over the railing of the ship? Did Lal, my other great-great—Samarsingh, and Bulaki crouch where they weren't supposed to, and in defiance of rules, roles, and fate, play cards, and did they finger their rudraksha beads while they watched storm after storm on the horizon form, ease each other's fears of the now sealed dis-entry back to India? Between Calcutta and Port of Spain did they aid and abet in the oceanic shifting concept of caste? Was a pundit always a pundit or did a man on board become Brahmin one day when the boat slid on a wave and slammed down? Amazed and grateful to be amongst the ones who survived, did he see the future and, in a flash, turn pundit?

My father, great-grandson of Bulaki, asserts: Everyone

is born a Hindu. Whether you like it or not

Not a pundit, but a Hindu

How you accessorize later is mortal prerogative

Brahmin

Breath

Au
  I O U
O
  I You We
M
  One for all and all for one
  All o' we
  Indivisible
  Is one

OK-OK, so it wasn't only the poor, the gullible, the unfortunate
the just-happened-to-be, who were recruited
Some, endowed with agency, just got the fuck out:
Things were bad; the British were there
Drought was there
The Sepoy so-called Mutiny—OK-OK, Rebellion, was there

One might be able to spin on one's heels three times
to become a Brahmin or wish upon a star
One can't do the same and become a pundit

A pundit, you see, must know Sanskrit
the Vedas, Ramayana, and the Bhagavad Gita—
none of which can be mastered convincingly
even on a bridge many times longer
hopping on the backs of monkeys
from India to Lanka

OK-OK, in hard times, even pundits can come upon hard times

OK-OK, so getting on a boat, even for a pundit, could have been a legit
line of escape

OK-OK, sorry, Bulaki Pundit. Just thinking

But Witnesses, what did you know? You had seen the Chinese come. The Germans. The Irish. A Scotsman here, a Scotsman there. Here there a Scotsman everywhere. You watched them leave. You saw the Africans distance themselves from donkey cart and cane field. Why did you not speak? What could you have told these ones who, surely you knew, would never return, pundit, golf caddy, sweet-drink and bottling manufacturer?

Witness, unbridle. Did you know my brother, descendant of pundit would fall so hard?
Poor boy, poor Indian boy, poor smart Indian boy
What Indian isn't still trying to climb out of indentureship?
Am I asking too much? Too much of you, eh Witness?

Samarsingh on board had a wife and seven-year-old son, Dipraj
Another jahaji bhai's wife was pregnant
The men bonded and Samarsingh's wife helped with the pregnant one
In jahaji solidarity, the unborn baby, if it was a girl, was promised as a
wife to the seven-year-old
When Samdia was nine, as good as gold, she and Dipraj were married

Dipraj and Samdia
My great-great-grandparents
Divine cause
Pinpoint effect

Three months after arriving on the sugar cane estate, the overseer pulled Bulaki from the work force because the labourer, he finds out, is actually a pundit. Bulaki becomes the El Dorado Estate pundit, administering to the cane farmers in Hindi and Bhojpuri.

Pundit's wife takes vegetables and provisions that are given to him in exchange for conducting pujas and she sells them roadside. She buys a cow. She sells the milk from the cow. She buys another cow. Sells more milk. Another cow. Eventually a car and employs an African man to drive the car as a taxi. Not too much later, she and her son buy a bus, soon a fleet of buses that prowl the route between Tunapuna and Port of Spain, an orange estate in the hills, a coconut estate on the Atlantic shore, and warehouses up and down the Port of Spain wharf.

Bulaki Pundit's great-grandson (my Daddy

2 4 6 8 by the College Gate eating roti from a plate)

studies medicine in Ireland, plays golf at the private club in Point-A-Pierre

(where)

Lal, an old man, now, caddies for my father.

Lal remembers a train station, steam, and the rumble of the train. Black swells heaving heavenward. Landmass of India receding. He does not recall the land itself. He was four. His grandparents, he proffers, are probably still waiting, wondering.

Sometimes, people disappear, he says. Just like that.

When I tell him All The Hindi I Know, his mouth opens as if to laugh his toothless gums glisten

Acha
Chalo
Aap ke naam kya hai?
Bayti Bayta
Meera Naam Shani Hai
Dhadi Dhada
Nahi
Hai

Do you know Hindi songs? Lal asks. I shake my head, no. He says, We didn't speak English or the patois the other people on the island spoke. We didn't mix with the African or the Chinee people, he says. Or the White people. The Puttagee or French. We spoke only Hindi and Bhojpuri. And you, he asks, You don't speak any Hindi or Bhojpuri? Only English? He wobbles his head and looks far-far away. So I tell him a story of a piece of cloth from India:

Kamarband, wound and wound about the waist, multi-tasking sash, essential of the Indian man, flamboyance quotidian—brow-mopper, money holder, grocery/letter carrier, pants cincher, dagger-hider

in translation, stationed in India, British armyman's borrow-theft—cummerbund—close, yes, and best with a cigar—heat mitigator, attribute enhancer, camouflager of imperfections in the aspiring man—conceals unflatterables: Tuxedo shirt's bunching buttons, wobbly bellies, rolling bands, too-tight trousers. Upturned pleats from artless lips indiscretions catch, and secret legitimate—and certainly illicit—calling cards

To explain—with learned pride and hilarity—my grandmother's white skin, this one-line: great grandmother, married to one Mr. Mathura, was the British estate owner's concubine

True or false? Close your eyes Witness. Some things we don't want to know. *But*

A minor detail: Kamarbanded Mathura with his bibi crossed the kala pani from his namesake province in Uttar Pradesh, birthplace of monsoon-cloud-blue Lord Krishna, where men like Mathura, and women like my great grandmother—stars in their honeyed eyes—are straight-nosed, poised, and pale—long preceding any god-damned "cross-the-kala-pani" estate owner

At formal dinners and dances, Bibi's Trinidad-born grandson (grandson, too, of Samdia and Dipraj, heir to the Suncrest Bottling Works Sweetdrink empire) outshone imperialist proprietorship of the ladder-climbed cummerbund

I, knee-high to a fly, from the arched verandah observed: Single-buttoned jacket dinner-jacket black, silk lapels, bow tie to match, shirt bright-bright light-exuding white, silky black stockings, and mirror-black shoes. Wavy hair patent-black, forehead garnished with provocative curl. Before getting behind the burled wheel of his burgundy Jaguar, Starboy, ring-adorned hand, smoothened upwards the pleats of his elevated MathuracityinthestateofUttarPradesh waistband. On leather heels honey-eyed-he spun—and voilà—a flash of dash—burgundy velvet-silk cummerbund

Is a short road from cutting cane with cutlass to cutting off a head with
the same   But OK OK   we surfacing black water, climbing
out cane field slowly in the olden days, the way out—after cutlass and
Gramoxone—used to be in the professions   but these days that slow
for so and it have easier and faster methods   and who don't respect
a gun better than a stethoscope?   This is the golden age of Trini
Demon Kings, Ravanas we, crack cocaine, chillum, and ganja
Up is up   no matter how you reach   sometimes is through the
barrel of a gun   And sometimes people disappear   just like that
You like my 24 ct yellow-yellow Aum and chain, golden like the
Indian sun?   Explain me why Indian always was the one cleaning
gutter   and when was the last time you see a Indian in my area
clean a gutter?   My mother not slaving over hot oil for a $2 doubles

She fanning sheself with
$$$$$$$$$$$$$$$$$$
from sales my crews on our corners bring in daily
We buying big car, no not car—
carzzz, not house—housezzz, boat, plane
All for one and one for all
So you use a privilege Indian to privilege a not-so-privilege Indian
whaz the big deal in dat?
A king on every other corner
Descendants of jahaji bhais, cousins all, we help one another

Doc where your son, he needing some?

Shootout in Sea Lots, Shootout in Cedros
In Gulf of Paria Bodies of Three More Found
Shootout in Maracas, Shootout in Las Cuevas
Shootout in Rio Claro, Shootout in Mayaro
Mother of Young Boy Killed in Gunfire Grieves:
Somebody, Wake Me Up From This Bad Dream

PM ADMITS
TENTACLES RUN DEEP
NO EASY FIX

Meanwhile, the Canada-born daughters of Indo-Trini immigrants to Toronto
In casual conversation and jest
Call their brothers *coolie*

In colder climes, no one bothers to bat an eye

How cool is that

2 4 6 8

Nevertheless, the roti shrank in size, rolled tightly, a stout cigar, pinned
with a toothpick whose end is festive frilled, curried chickpeas—not
channa—filled, (a dusting of amchar powder delivers subtle notes
of Chandni Chowk and fragrant hints of ancestry) displayed on
a fig-leaf-lined plate (for ole-times' sake) surrounded by Pride of
Barbados flowers, the roti's name now preceded by "cocktail," met
with a cappella'd ooohs and aaahs. Manicured hands of a variety of
shades outstretch for a little piece of

2 4 6 8

Witness, oh Witness, when is a transgression not a transgression?

Thus spake Witness:

Pundit, Caddy, Businessman, Teacher, Street sweeper
Poopa, Mooma, Nani, Nana, Kaki, Kaka, Bhowji, Chachi
brother, sister, drug dealer, jahaji bhai

Child

Indo-Caribbean duennes
Black water hear-say
Impaled on estates—whose names you don't even know
Bagasse bequest
Cutlass cum gun-coolie
Toted in the illusory
Unattainable
Fantasy of authenticity

Accept the facts, nah:

Agricultural Indentureship begun in 1845, ended in 1917

But the covenant, colonialism's metastatic legacy

Indentureship emotional, Indentureship mental

Ergo, EveryIndianman's back plays host to a monkey

Ey, listen, Neighbour-neighbour, wey yuh dey?

(Gun-shot interrupting)

Shut up your mouth
Who gets the money—
Is what is all about

Time to deal
Deliver the boy another round

And hear me good:
Stay wey you dey
I climb your back

Not the other way

Wondrous Cold

Wondrous Cold

i.
Some insist you and I are made
In the specific likeness of a supposed god

>   Once upon an atom time
>   We were oh-so elegant

Seasons of water—
Water, water, anyhow—

Ice is a coming skin of the earth

>   "Wondrous," Mr. Coleridge?

Indeed, it has, everywhere, "grown wondrous cold"

And wondrous hot

>   Vast areas of swampy coniferous taiga
>   unrecoverable natural carbon sink peatland
>   flame-devoured
>   wildfire smoke
>   plumes the North Pole
>   heat-absorbing particulates deposited
>   melting Arctic Circle sea ice
>   emitting 188 megatonnes
>   of carbon

If you're living in a low-income developing country—uh, well, good luck!

Not all, but those who can afford
Afford and afford
Technology

                              gratification today
                              rots us tomorrow

Zip up shiny skins
Pop a synthetic against
Air pollution from wildfire smoke
Deadening cold and winds that kill

                              And expect to endure

The castles we have built:
Nuclear, biological, chemical

                              weaponry
Decline in bee and bat biodiversity
Pandemics bioengineered
Guns and bump stocks
The catastrophic climatic changes we have steered

Aware of consequences, we're yet like addicts
                    Remorseful yesterday, today we forget
Quench our insatiable hunger
For the real thing:

Antler, bear bladder, tiger bone, rhino horn, tusk, tail, liver, kidney, pelt,
feather, claw, musk deer gland, black bear bile, tiger penis, lion bone,
pink dolphin, pangolin, iguana, Japanese macaque, pig, buffalo, horse,
alligator, crocodile, dog, snake, ostrich, kangaroo, yak, cow, sheep,
goat, mink, fox, cat, coyote, wolf, rabbit, deer, caterpillar, sea horse,
pheasant, partridge, wild turkey, gazelle, elephant, gorilla, African
grey parrot, lemur, orangutan, macaw, turtledove, Eurasian goldfinch,
European roller, red-backed shrike, hawksbill sea turtle, tortoise

ii.
Were I phytoplankton—

Marine magician
Converter of light and liquid air
Supreme preserver of oxygen
Benefactor of environments not its own

Were I phytoplankton—

Zooplankton's share
Sacrificial of shrimp baleen duck and jellyfish

Were I phytoplankton—

Excitable fluorescence
Shape-shifting aquatic constellation

—I might cop centre stage
Now and long beyond the notion of After

iii.
No precision or gospel for this recreant
No God, no moment of *Oh God!* here

Purpose devotion mission—
High-minded and charlatanical-subterfuge
of the sheeple by the sheeple (supposedly for the sheeple)

    No God
    To praise
    Or blame
For magnificent accidents of consequence

Sorry, but there's just us…

        I believe in the Almighty Accident
        Creator of all Universe and beyond
        Moon, sun, heat, gravity, and velocity
        O, Co2, H2O, orchid lava gold bone
        Exploding stars and piper nigrum

The basic instinctual will of lust-
ful molecules
To gyrate tremble whirl re-solve
To multiply like bunnies and W. Churchill's Indians
To distort modify adapt and habituate

To compete (or should that be thrive)
Against (or should that be in) ever-morphing environs

Admittedly if there's to be no God
No moment of *Oh God*
Where are the broken lines along which to tear
      lines to not cross?

iv.
This mind, this brain, fingers, toes
Blood and heart, music in the veins and photographs
The birds at the beating heartland of me

Caretaker of those birds—
Were it not for her and them then what of this
Haphazard crush and entwine of atom et al?

One of us may die first, and the other will come to know
What she'd long ago intuited: that love, too, is subterfuge

The lies we tend
We harness to produce meaning

v.
Let skin heart lungs stomach
Liver kidney intestines brain
Of every brand and manner of living thing
Embrace

Cancerdroughtearthquakefrostbitehungerhurricanehyperthermia
pandemicpestilencesinkholetsunamivolcano

We could, of course, do something

                        Goddamit, do something! Fast!

But those whose profits will be eaten into
Will have to have a heart

             That's how the crumbling of the cookie got its start

The castles we built imprisoned
And are now falling
On us

But how smart "we" once were to have tapped gas
Burned the fossils
Laid down pipelines
Siphoned it into our homes, and kept
Those cooking and warming fires burning burning burning

Game of Watch the Migrant Dream #1

PROLOGUE
Destination

At your service   masterful dreamer   (in need of a job)
          doesn't do just anything   for a pittance
                    but your pleasure primary of course
                    she dreams   as Migrants often do
          (yes, some will charge you less   but not all dreams
                    and wanderers are created...)

                    You may, as you will
                              take notes
                              pictures

PERFORMANCE
The Recurring Dream

Plane of the recurring dream—itinerants aboard!

The airplane of the recurring dream travels
an asphalt highway
built on stilts, a flyway of solid ground

The acceleration of the recurring dream
is as fast as the speed of the plane:
nose preceding, body angled, rising...

Back wheels remain riveted
to solid ground.

In the temple of the recurring dream, travel is horizontal—
liftoff and arrival, like belief, are suspended.

Passengers become occupants
drifters from seat to seat
their motion unceasing—
seat belts buckled, unbuckled, buckled—
mesmerized window-seat watchers
while landmarks blur: tree, stone, concrete

In the plane of dreams
liftoff is unexpected
there's no pilot, no flight crew

Destination:
necessarily unattended
comfortably unattained

Game of Watch the Migrant Dream #2

PROLOGUE

Abyss fissure chasm canyon crevasse crack

On one side note-takers abundant
pencil they   notepad in hand

On the other side, Migrant she   rope-ladder
intention to cross, in tow

One side bugle calls
signals start   of this performance

PERFORMANCE:
Another Recurring Dream

i

Gathered up rope-ladder   Migrant swings swing
                    Swing swing swing
            She flings   F   L   I   NG
            Rope hits one side, note-takers roar

        Oh god rope slipping   slippery slope

            Crowd coaxes Migrant's rope
        note-takers squeal but rope a metre short
        pulled back back and slips slowly off
            off by its own weight, imagine!

        Note-takers take notes   too busy, of course
                    and pictures (to be sure)
                    busy busy busy
    but Migrant she   proud Migrant dreaming   proud she
            takes rope-hauling   like a course
        retrieves hope dangling (par for the course)

        Abyss fissure chasm canyon crevasse crack

ii

Once re-gathered rope-ladder bugle calls
swing swing swing swing swing swingswung

Doing the Migrant fling (momentum, to be sure!)
F   L   I   NG

Rope (at least this) arrives one side, bigger uproar
      But   and   but   rose lips

Crowd analysis:
Migrant's materials methods nature nurture, to be sure!
Dream a metre short, damn oh dear
(its very own weight length — imagine!) lips lowly off

Note-takers watch   Migrant hauling   hope
busy busy busy no takers watch

She Migrant this   Migrant fling   ing
    Dream   other side dreaming
Inch by inch   hours of haul   hope as long as deep as

Abyss fissure chasm canyon crevasse crack

iii

renewed   undeterred   rope-ladder   swing
     swings   wingswungsungsungswingswing
     swung   Momentum achieved, whose for sure?
       FL   I   NG
                 falls

far from one side different crowd bigger furor
some uh uhs no buts no ands no oars
crowd hoaxes   rope squeals a metre short
so much for hauling weigh (imagine that, its
own its weight) lips lowly slips solely it's another
Migrant falling another Migrant mauling for sure

Point of Convergence

union of backhome
way back then, and home

where *I* depend neither
on memory nor desire
where *I* am neither
mendhi, baigan, steelpan

nor mindless of these

it's a seamless concoction
like mulligatawny: cooks long and slow
neither jeera, cardamom, hurdi
nor clove
stand alone

it's hybridity
as in: "offspring of tame sow and wild boar
child of freeman and slave"
some new stew
or callaloo

spotted variegated deformed crude
new

Calcottawarima
persimango-orangegrapepear
Vancouverlaromainottawa
pommeracapplepommecythere

where neither Nepalese great-grandmother
nor mother, lover, government
define *I*

nor am *I*
mindless of these

Cosmic

Cosmic

///

This body-epic is an origami finger game
Each quadrant
        India, Ireland, Trinidad, Canada
A miniseries on the Ferris wheel and fall
Of a globalized
        commodified-by-history-performed-by-me
Existence

Chaotic flap of wings, liftoff
        synonymous with *separation*
From the nub
        synchronous with *refuge*
Of family

Emigration equals
        pulling out the big guns
Evading sweet and sour subterfuge

Saturday evenings
        fried chicken livers, onions, Afong's hops
                a panman practicing for tomorrow's jump-up

Sunday kiskadees and dogs howling, 5 am
        scents of hours spent (knock on the door)
                in bathrooms (knock on the door)
                        newspaper ink (knock on the door)
                                perfumed soap (knock on the door) conflating

Neighbour, neighbour, wey yuh dey?
Eyes like flies, watching-watching
Maco fuh so, but is true, is you
Who did see and call police
For tief, tief breaking down we back door

///

Sifting the intimate from the public
Of all that *backhome* girds
Is to be anointed   by dust

Of an expanding   universe
To ride   its coattail   unhinged
Freed from the ubiquitous noose of
      Well, that's-just-how-it's-always-been-done

     The village that brought up the child
     Expects its ton of flesh

Walls listen
It is the rare one who isn't foraging for evil

On your mark, get set *go*
everybody is a radio

///

In Cosmopolita, neighbours do not belong
Should eyes meet, nod, but noncommittally
To be un-considered is to be under the radar

News reporters enquire, neighbours answer:
But he was always such a quiet man
Never said a word to anyone
Who would have thunk it, eh?

Climb a mountain, fall from grace
You're on your own
Come as you are, leave as you please
You're on your own
Bring home whom and what you dare

You're on your own
Cosmopolita, isn't it grand
Work yourself to the bone
No one gives a damn
You want what you want
You can die in front of the tv alone

///

Wanderlust shoots elephants (FE 70–200mm f/2.8) in Sri Lanka
Anticipates cobras in thousands-of-years-old Indian Buddhist caves
Listens for Nichiren and Shijo Kingo parsing life
       the dress code, perhaps, of the samurai in Mt. Fuji's shadow
On a boat on the Bosporus, air thick like suzme
          wanderlust contemplates living in the dusk
          of mosques that once were churches

Barbeques kangaroo fillets (three minutes per side, at most) in
Australia
Hikes in the Sierra Madre in Mexico
       so many greens here, announces the khaki-clad American
Ponders what wisdom in Frankfurt churns art and music
       out of the IG Farben Building
Observes the flow of men in white dresses
         through a Perpignan Maghrebi neighbourhood
         during Muslim salat times
Toasts Karen in Spain
       with three kinds of vermouth

In Panama kingfishers dart down then back up the narrow river
Off Osa in Costa Rica I await the capsizing of the boat
       certain I am to die by drowning

Hawaii, I wished I were there with someone else

In Martinique I kept my eyes closed
       because I knew if I opened them
       you wouldn't be there

///

The Varanus water monitor named Ali Douyoung
Is the revered spiritual sister of the son
Of the south Sulawesi Bugis Abdul Halim

Tsuruko Hanzawa dresses in a ceremonial kimono
Travels in her van across Japan
Practicing the art of kaiseki cuisine, serving tea
To anyone who sits long enough for ceremony

"Wet-hulled" sounds the same as "wet-processed" but is different
Giling Basah (wet-hulled) specific to Indonesia, creates a signature
flavor
More body, lower acidity. The beans require longer drying in the roaster

Siniuss (Blue Snake) and Truuvar (Loyal Man)
Fought alongside their brother Rahurikkuja (Troublemaker) a.k.a. Rurik
of Lagoda
Who founded the Rurik dynasty (862) in Novgorod
And ruled all of Kievan Rus

I Google past lovers
And mourn with Omar Sharif
At the funeral of Oum Kalthoum

A bird in the hand requires beat-steady dancing to the music of the
Amazigh

My cupboards host Balsamic di Modena, cinnamon di Sri Lanka
Vanilla di Mexico, saffron di Spain

Loose tea di Nuwara Eliya
Green coffee di Sumatra, Honduras, and Colombia

Viva Viva
Palestina
  Song of goodwill
  Splinter in the heart

Backhome I inform the maid of her rights
Encourage her to fight for those rights
  (when I leave I take her net with me)

///

During pandemic lockdowns
I design my own shoes, handmade in Italy
The blink of an eye from order to delivery
Come shawls and table linen, from Sarajevo and India
Matcha and artisan bowls direct—no middle man—from Japan
The world is a *PayPal* fingertip and a day or two away

Friends, family, and strangers
Popping in for a Zoomed hour or two—no more
            no dishes to wash
From Vancouver to Halifax
Brazil, England, Argentina, Trinidad, the USA

Global, I, my circles and friends, we surely are

///

Round and round the globe, global we are, here we come
There we go—plane travel for that two-week getaway in the sun
      (guzzles fossil fuels, spews carbon, cooks the planet)
Cruising the coast to Juneau, Alaska)
      (dumps approx. 8 tons of raw sewage
      per week
      into the highway of ocean)

The original globalization: empire expansion
Today's iteration: Russia's WAR on Ukraine
      (causes fuel and food shortages in Asia, Africa, Eastern
      Europe, and the Pacific)
European dependence on Russian gas and oil
      (funds Putin's mass murder in his WAR on Ukraine)

Spectator wars weave through the news
      Yemen and Saudi Arabia, Tigre, Eritrea and Ethiopia, DRC, Syria...
We've got the whole world   in our hands
We've got the whole world   in our hands
      all the channels at our command

That same tour-the-world Internet: Bethlehem of Conspiracists
Cathedral of misinformation, hackers, fact deniers, truth distorters
      is the House of the Dictator and Autocrat

Furnishes the taste for the exotic
(West Coast salmon, caught off B.C., smoked in Lithuania
sent back for sale in Canada)
Precursor of extinction
Unregulated farming of animals for higher-priced consumption
Civets, sturgeon, and Beluga caviar
Will set us apart, your global from my global
And trap us in the isolation of hula-hoop pandemics

Now that's cosmic

///

During the three-day misdiagnosis of cancer
There is no family nearby
(to worry about, trouble, and upset)

One has time to oneself
To plan, to cry, to regret

No one to hold on to, to hold you
To slice bread, make tea
To tell you what you should and shouldn't do

No one knocked on the door
You read the news on the Internet
In impolite peace

Notes and Acknowledgements

Notes

Inglan: A Green and Pleasant Land

"Inglan," as dubbed by Linton Kwesi Johnson in "Inglan Is a Bitch."

Thomas Picton was a British Army officer and governor of Trinidad who was known for his cruelty, particularly the torture of a fourteen-year-old girl, Luisa Calderón. Picton in Prince Edward County where I live is named after him.

In 1808, William Blake wrote the poem "And did those feet in ancient time," the last line of which is: "In England's green and pleasant Land." The poem was set to music in 1916 by Sir Hubert Parry and is known now as "Jerusalem." It is considered an unofficial second national anthem in England.

"This precious stone set in the silver sea" is borrowed from John of Gaunt's speech in *Richard II* by William Shakespeare.

In 2022, the late Queen's lady-in-waiting, Lady Susan Hussey, insisted to know from British-born activist Ngozi Fulani where she was "really from." According to Fulani, Hussey, eventually satisfied, said: "Ha! I knew we'd get there in the end, you're Caribbean!"

Brown Girl in The Ring

The lines "They traded with us and gave us everything they had… and are gentle and always laughing" are excerpted from the *Diary of Christopher Columbus Baldwin, Librarian of the American Antiquarian Society, 1829–1835.*

In 1995, modeller Alan Maslankowski was given the task of creating a Royal Doulton figurine of Christopher Columbus to honor the 500th anniversary of the discovery of the New World.

Bartolomé

The full title of Bartolomé de las Casas's travelogue is as follows: *A Brief Account of the Destruction of the Indies; Or, a faithful NARRATIVE OF THE Horrid and Unexampled Massacres, Butcheries, and all manner of Cruelties, that Hell and Malice could invent, committed by the Popish Spanish Party on the inhabitants of West-India, TOGETHER With the Devastations of several Kingdoms in America by Fire and Sword, for the space of Forty and Two Years, from the time of its first Discovery by them.*

Bartolomé de las Casas has been proposed for canonization in the Roman Catholic Church.

The Nevertheless Queen

Queen Isabella was canonized by the Catholic Church as a "servant of God" in 1974, but the process was reconsidered in 1991 due to her expulsion of Jewish people. In April 2020, Pope Francis asked to reopen the request for the canonization of Isabella.

Matayla, Matayla

When I was a very young child I lived with my grandparents on Sutton Street in San Fernando, Trinidad. Twice a day, a woman we called Matayla passed by on the road in front of our house. I don't know anyone who had ever actually spoken to her, or who knew anything about her. Images of her and questions about her have haunted me. She was, in fact, the person who inspired my Mala in *Cereus Blooms at Night*.

We

First appeared in *Wasafiri* 110, "Afterlives of Indenture," May 2022.

Reproduced here from my first poetry collection *The Predicament of Or*, published by Polestar Book Publishers in 2001, are four poems: embedded in the title poem is "All the Hindi I Know," and standing on their own are "Game of Watch the Migrant Dream #1," "Game of Watch the Migrant Dream #2" and "Point of Convergence." More than twenty years after that collection was published, I remain as concerned as I was back then about issues I had alluded to, among them immigration, displacements of peoples, hybrid identities, how and who we love, and how we navigate visibility and invisibility.

Witness, Oh Witness Dey!

First published in *Candice Lin: Pigs and Poison*, Govett-Brewster Art Gallery, 2022.

Acknowledgements

I would like to acknowledge my debt to the writers, artists, and filmmakers who have come before me, who are with me now, and who propelled me onward into what became *Oh Witness Dey!* They have been my witnesses and I theirs. Among them are: Savi Naipaul Akal, *The Naipauls of Nepaul Street,* Felipe Fernández-Armest, *1492: The Year the World Began*, Gaiutra Bahadur, *Coolie Woman: The Odyssey of Indenture*, Marina Carter and Khal Torabully, *Coolitude: An Anthology of the Indian Labour Diaspora*, Eduardo Galeano, *Open Veins of Latin America: Five Centuries of the Pillage of a Continent*, Harold Sonny Ladoo, *No Pain Like This Body*, Candice Lin, *Pigs and Poison,* Canisia Lubrin, *The Dyzgraphxst: A Poem*, Colin M. MacLachlan, *Spain's Empire in the New World: The Role of Ideas in Institutional and Social Change*, Patricia Mohammed, *Gender Negotiations Among Indians in Trinidad, 1917–1947: Springer*, Olasupo Shasore, *Journey of an African Colony* (Documentary series), Deborah Root, *Cannibal Culture: Art, Appropriation, and the Commodification of Difference,* Olive Senior, *Hurricane Watch: New and Collected Poems*, Derek Walcott, *Omeros*, and Derek Walcott and Peter Doig, *Morning, Paramin.*

This current collection of poems began when curator Rosa Tyhurst and Spike Island Gallery director Robert Leckie commissioned the poem that would become "Witness, Oh Witness Dey" for the catalogue for Candice Lin's travelling exhibition Pigs and Poison. On seeing that poem, Andil Gosine and Nalini Mohabir requested another from me for *Wasafiri* 110, Afterlives of Indenture, which they were editing. For them, I wrote "We." These two poems, "We" and "Witness, Oh Witness Dey," were the impetus for a year-long immersion in and expansion of the ideas therein, and to them all—to Rosa, Robert, Candice, Andil and Nalini, I owe a huge thanks.

I would like to thank Lang Baker, Winston Dookeran, Richard Fung, Marlene MacCallum, Shelagh Mathers, David Morrish, and Sandra

Ridley for reading this manuscript, whether in part or in full, and making generous and insightful comments, and for their friendship and encouragement.

Without the support of my siblings Vahli Mahabir, Ramesh Mootoo Jr., Indrani Mootoo, and Kavir Mootoo, these creative pursuits in which I engage would be hollow. Thank you, Mootoos, for reading, for your comments, and so much more. Thank you, also, Kavir, for allowing the use of your artwork in the design of the book's cover.

Colonial histories and the politics of representation being Deborah Root's area of specialty, she plied me, in her excitement about what I was writing, with pertinent and fascinating texts and engaged me in the most interesting and eye-opening conversations on an almost daily basis. Thank you, Deborah, for these ongoing riches and delights.

It was my fortune to have had this book edited by the learned creative thinker and poet Shazia Hafiz Ramji. Your rigour and diligence, Shazia, were a real treasure. And the same with scholar Ramabai Espinet. The care with which you, Ramabai, as consulting editor, attended to the book was exacting, detailed, and, given the material, vital. Thank you, Ramabai. These few lines of gratitude do not adequately convey the importance I place in the editing phase, and in particular this one, wherein conversations with these two brilliant minds one's own was constantly sent soaring in unexpected directions.

Mistakes and errors made in a text that is as joyfully contemptuous of conventions as this one may appear deliberate to a reader. I am in awe of the work of copy editor Jo Ramsay, and that of proofreader Laurie Siblock. A shoutout that cannot be loud enough to them both for their brilliant talents and skills.

Not least, thank you to all at Book*hug Press—Charlene Chow, Gareth Lind, Reid Millar, Sabrina Papas, and to publishers Hazel Millar and Jay MillAr for once again so attentively and generously supporting my work.

Photo: Darren Rampersad

About the Author

Shani Mootoo was born in Ireland and raised in Trinidad. Mootoo's highly acclaimed writing includes the novels *Polar Vortex*, *Moving Forward Sideways Like a Crab*, *Valmiki's Daughter*, *He Drown She in the Sea*, and *Cereus Blooms at Night* (which is now a Penguin Classic and a Vintage Classic), as well as the poetry collections *The Predicament of Or* and *Cane I Fire*. Her poetry has appeared in *Wasafiri*, *Poetry Magazine*, and *Room Magazine*. She has been awarded the degree of Doctor of Letters honoris causa from Western University, is a recipient of Lambda Literary's James Duggins Outstanding Mid-Career Novelist Prize, and the Writers' Trust Engel Findley Award. She lives in Southern Ontario, Canada.

Colophon

Manufactured as the first edition of
Oh Witness Dey!
in the spring of 2024 by Book*hug Press

Edited for the press by Shazia Hafiz Ramji
Consulting Editor: Ramabai Espinet
Copy-edited by Jo Ramsay
Proofread by Laurie Siblock
Cover artwork: Kavir Mootoo
with an illustration by iStock.com/GeorgePeters
Design and typesetting by Gareth Lind, Lind Design
Typeset in Trade Gothic Next (Jackson Burke/Akira Kobayashi,
1948/2008) and Canturiana (Latinotype, 2022)

Printed in Canada

bookhugpress.ca